LIFE IN THE
POLAR LANDS

Monica Byles

Consultant Roger Hammond
Director of Living Earth

SCHOLASTIC INC.
New York Toronto London Auckland Sydney

ISBN 0-590-46130-3

Copyright © 1990 by Two-Can Publishing Ltd. All rights reserved. Published by Scholastic Inc., 730 Broadway, New York, NY 10003, by arrangement with Two-Can Publishing Ltd.

12 11 10 9 8 7 6 5 4   2 3 4 5 6 7/9

Printed in the U.S.A.   09

First Scholastic printing, January 1993

Photograph Credits:
p. 4 (top) NHPA/Stephen Kraseman p.4/5 NHPA/Gordon Claridge p.7 Survival Anglia/Joel Bennett p.8 Ardea/Clem Haagner p.10 (top) Survival Anglia/Rick Price (bottom) B. & C. Alexander p.11 (top) Ardea (bottom) Ardea/Jean-Paul Ferrero p.12 Ardea/E. Mickleburgh p.13 (top) Ardea/Ron & Valerie Taylor (bottom) NHPA/Stephen Krasemann p.14 Bruce Coleman/Inigo Everson p.15 (top) Survival Anglia/Rick Price (bottom) Ardea/François Gohier p.16 B. & C. Alexander p.19 Bruce Coleman/Norbert Rosling p.20/21 Survival Anglia/Colin Willock p.21 Bruce Coleman/E. & P. Bauer p.22 NHPA/Peter Johnson p.23 B. & C. Alexander/Robert Estall
Front cover: Seaphot/Planet Earth/Howard Platt Back cover: Tony Stone Worldwide

Illustrations by Francis Mosley. Edited by Claire Watts. Artworking by Claire Legemah.

CONTENTS

Looking at the Poles	4
Where in the world	6
Frozen features	8
Animal life	10
Birdland	12
Sea life	14
People of the Poles	16
Watching the weather	18
Exploiting the Poles	20
Saving the Poles	22
Crow steals some daylight	24
True or false?	29
Glossary	30
Index	32

LOOKING AT THE POLES

Few areas in the world are as harsh and desolate as the North and South Poles and few are as beautiful. For much of the year both areas are freezing cold, with fierce winds and thick snow and ice on the ground. As it grows colder even the seas freeze.

Not many animals live here. Some species, however, are hardy enough to live, breed, and find food in the open wastes. Their bodies have specially adapted to the constant cold.

In the summer months, May to July at the North Pole and November to January at the South Pole, the sun shines even at midnight. In winter, the Poles remain almost permanently dark.

The snow and ice recede in the short summers, leaving the ground littered with pools of **meltwater**. The land is covered with flowers and bursts of green leaves. Creatures mate and nest or find safe places to give birth to their young. The air is filled with insects.

► Plants in the polar lands spend most of the time under snow but burst into life during the short summer. Their seeds are very hardy and do not **germinate** until the conditions around them are exactly right for growth.

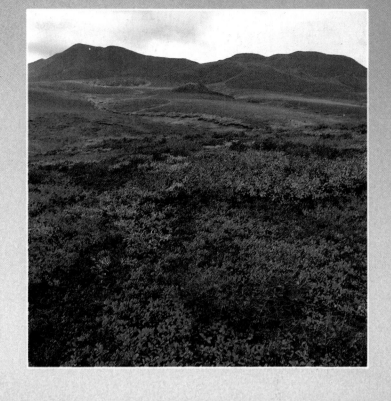

▼ A large **iceberg** floats in the summer sea off Antarctica. It is sunset but at this time of year the sky never really grows dark.

WHERE IN THE WORLD

The Poles are at the top and bottom of the earth. As they are farther from the sun than any other point on the earth, the sun's rays are weaker, which makes the polar lands colder than anywhere else in the world.

At the North Pole lies a frozen sea, called the Arctic Ocean. This ocean is surrounded by northern Europe, the Soviet Union, and North America. The most northerly point where trees will grow is about 2,300 km (1,429 miles) from the North Pole. In between the **treeline** and the **icecap**, lie regions of **tundra**, which is rough terrain covered with rugged vegetation. The layer of earth beneath the tundra is always frozen, even in summer. It is called **permafrost**.

The continent of Antarctica lies at the South Pole, and is permanently covered in a thick shield of ice. Snow

HISTORY OF THE POLES

150–170 million years ago

The Poles are not frozen. The South Pole may lie over low ground and the North Pole over open ocean.

60–70 million years ago

Shifts in the earth's plates cause the Poles to move to the positions where they now lie. They begin to cool and some of the original animal species are unable to adapt to the new conditions.

5–6 million years ago

Polar lands are still quite warm at sea-level. Changes in the climate and in the heat received from the sun bring new conditions of snow and ice which have been there ever since.

NORTH POLE FACTS

● Because the North Pole is surrounded by land, warmer currents from close to the equator never reach the Arctic Ocean to warm it.

● The Ancient Greeks named the Arctic after the constellation of the Great Bear, which they called Arktos.

● Robert Peary and Matthew Henson were the first European people to reach the North Pole in 1909.

and ice lie deeper here than anywhere else in the world.

The Poles were not always such cold places. Fossils of trees, plants, and animals found in Antarctica show that it once had a much warmer climate. Movements of the **plates** that make up the earth's surface, together with the

▲ A herd of caribou pass along the northern treeline on their annual journey to richer feeding grounds.

warming and cooling of our planet over many centuries, have finally brought about the chilly conditions we know at the Poles today.

SOUTH POLE FACTS

South Atlantic

South America

SOUTH POLE

Indian Ocean

Antarctic Circle

South Pacific

● 75 percent of the world's water is stored in glaciers and most of this lies in the Antarctic icecap.

● The Antarctic can be called a desert as it receives less than 150mm (6 inches) of rain or snow per year.

● Norwegian Roald Amundsen beat Britain's Robert Scott to the South Pole by one month in 1911.

FROZEN FEATURES

A quarter of the world's oceans and seas are affected by ice every year. Most of this comes in the form of icebergs. An Antarctic iceberg has reached almost as far north as Rio de Janeiro, a long journey of 5,500km (3,440 miles).

At the South Pole, ice covers the land and forms cliffs and glaciers. As the ice in the glaciers becomes old and heavy, it moves slowly forward and reaches the sea after many years. Long tongues of this glacier extend out into the sea and large chunks of ice break off. This ice floats away to become brand new icebergs.

◀ Paradise Bay Glacier in the Antarctic. Sections break off from these craggy cliffs and plummet into the clear waters below to form new icebergs.

Icebergs are made from frozen fresh water but at the Poles the salty ocean freezes too. This reaches a peak in February and March when there is about 12 million km^2 (4.5 million square miles) of sea-ice in the Arctic Ocean and 3 million km^2 (1 million square miles) off Antarctica.

As the sea freezes, a greasy film appears to cover the water. A curtain of wispy "smoke" rises from the surface and, as the sea water turns to ice, salt is pushed above the surface in beautiful crystals called **ice flowers**.

Ever since the sinking of the ocean liner *The Titanic* by an iceberg in 1912, losing 1,522 lives, the International Ice Patrol has kept watch on icebergs to alert shipping to possible danger in the ocean.

DIFFERENT SORTS OF ICE

● **Tabular icebergs** have broken off from ice shelves. They have flat tops and are sometimes used by scientists as convenient research bases.

● As the sea freezes the first ice to form is not very solid. It is called **frazil ice**. As the salt content is pushed out thick **pancake ice** forms. Finally slabs of ice freeze together to form **pack ice**.

● Glacier bergs have broken off glaciers that run into the sea. This is dense, ancient ice. As it is so heavy, only about one-tenth shows above the water's surface.

● Fragments of ice are called **brash ice**. Large fragments from the **ice sheet** are called **bergy bits** and smaller pieces are known as **growlers**.

ANIMAL LIFE

Despite the bleakness of the polar lands, many animals live there, either all year around or as summer visitors when the temperature rises to 10°C (50°F) above freezing.

On the Antarctic ice sheet most of the permanent residents are insects. On the very edge of the ice there are penguins, seals, and migratory birds, while the sea is filled with an abundance of life.

An enormous variety of animals live in the Arctic Circle, from the tiny shrew to the huge polar bear. Native species are well adapted to make use of the short summer and protect themselves against the long winter. Polar animals tend to be larger than their similar cousins in warmer climates. They have short legs, long hair, and an undercoat

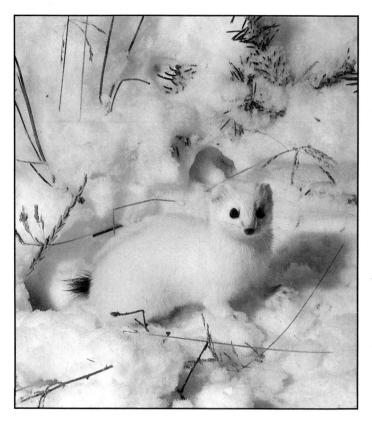

▲ The stoat, like many other animals, grows a white **pelt** during the winter. This helps to **camouflage** him against the snow when hunting.

▼ Polar bear cubs are born in pairs and stay with their mother for up to two years. Polar bears may live up to 33 years in the wild.

▶ Seals come in many shapes and sizes. They are superbly adapted to a life in and out of water. Seals are torpedo-shaped to help them glide easily through the water. Their bodies are covered in a thick layer of **blubber** which protects their internal organs from the cold. This blubber is between 2.5 and 15 cm (1–6 inches) thick and gives seals energy when there is no food available.

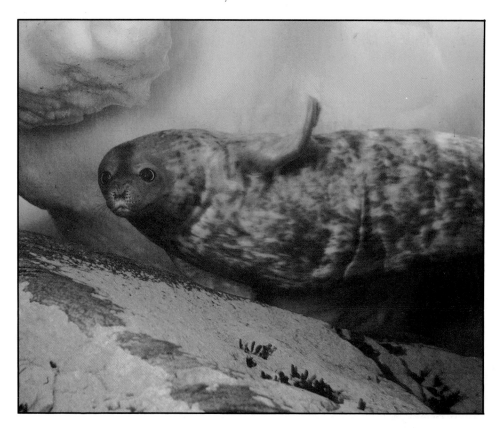

of dense fur. Their tails are short and the pads on their large feet are furry.

Every 10 to 13 years small mammals such as lemmings or voles breed in enormous numbers. With such a ready supply of food available, larger carnivores also grow in number. Eventually there is little vegetation for the small mammals to eat and many of them die. The larger animals then also suffer a large population drop and the vegetation begins to grow back.

◀ A pack of wolves follow their leader into the treeline. A wolf can see and smell its prey over 1.6 km (one mile) away. Most wolves have gray fur but the Arctic wolf may grow pure white fur for camouflage against the snow.

Wolves can eat up to 9 kg (20 pounds) of food at one time. However, they can go without eating for two weeks or longer.

BIRDLAND

The polar winter is too cold for most birds, but during the summer many species of birds arrive. The Arctic tern flies from summer at one Pole to summer at the other. It covers a distance of 30,000 km (18,750 miles) every year. Other birds include geese, duck such as widgeon, eider, and teal, as well as smaller birds such as larks and pipits. On the surface lie pools of melted ice and snow where millions of mosquitoes and other insects flourish. The humming air is a feast for birds!

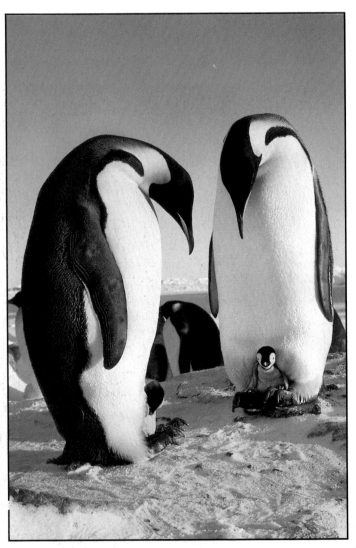

During the winter, a number of birds live on the **subarctic** wastes of the tundra where they survive by searching for roots and berries under the snow or by feeding on other birds, small mammals, or insects. Here in the north live the ptarmigan, the snowy owl and, close to the treeline, the raven and Arctic redpoll.

Throughout the Antarctic year, birds such as penguins remain hardy in all conditions. A penguin can dive as deep as 50 m (164 feet) underwater in search of fish. This is the height of a 24-story building! King penguins must return to land every five to six weeks during the winter to feed their growing young. The adults then cluster together on the shore, the cold penguins from the edge of the group exchanging places with the warmed birds from the center every few minutes. Their young soon grow into enormous brown furry lumps of some 12 kg (26 pounds) in body weight, but have to fast for up to a month at a time while their parents are out at sea. By the spring, they weigh no more than 6 kg (13 pounds). Many chicks die during this period.

◄ The largest of the penguin family is the emperor. It stands over 1 m (3 feet) tall and weighs up to 40 kg (90 pounds). The male penguin **incubates** the eggs in a special pouch on his feet. He will go as long as two months without eating.

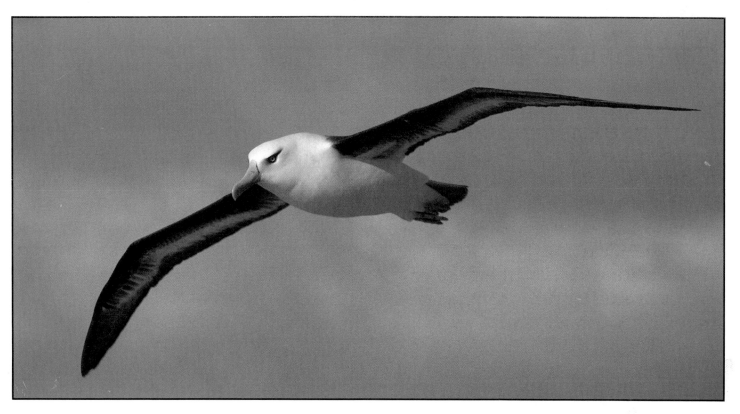

▲ A black-browed albatross flies over the Southern Ocean. It has long thin wings which help it to glide through the air.

▼ Puffins fly to the Arctic circle during the summer and nest among the rocky cliffs surrounding the frozen ocean.

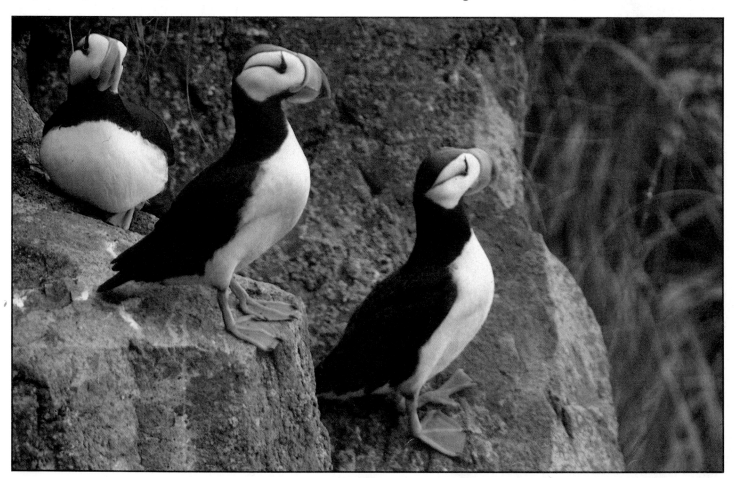

SEA LIFE

Below the waves and ice of the polar oceans, the temperature remains far more constant than at the surface. For this reason, creatures such as polar bears, seals, and penguins prefer to spend as much time as possible diving and swimming.

In the Antarctic the stable temperature and warm currents from more temperate zones encourage many varieties of colorful growth. Bright orange sea spiders, delicate anemones, fronds of primitive weeds, worms, and other strange creatures litter the sea floor.

Strange ghostly fish live here too, like the pale ice-fish or transparent deep-sea angler. In areas under the ice where little light filters through to

ARCTIC FOODCHAIN

toothed whale

large **carnivores** eat small carnivores

seals

small carnivores eat **herbivores**

fish

herbivores eat plants and simple animals

plankton

This is a foodchain of polar animals living in the sea. Smaller animals tend to be eaten by larger animals. Herbivores eat only plants or simple life such as krill. At the bottom of the chain, plants and simple animals do not need to eat major organisms to stay alive.

◀ Krill are tiny crustaceans similar to shrimps. Some countries, including Japan, have recently begun fishing for krill to provide food for people. This mass harvesting of krill poses a threat to the creatures of the polar lands which rely on them as a primary food source.

the depths, these creatures have no need of bright coloring. Many carry an internal light source, supplied by bacteria carried in a special gland.

The largest marine animals, the whales, live mainly in the Antarctic zone. Biggest of all are the blue whales which grow up to 30 m (98 feet) long and weigh 150,000 kg (14.8 tons). They are the largest animals on earth. There are two groups of whales: **toothed whales**, which feed on fish and seals, and **baleen whales**, which feed on tiny creatures called krill. Baleen whales have a series of bony plates in their mouths which help them sift the krill from the water.

▶ A killer whale breaching. Killer whales are in fact members of the dolphin family. They can swim as fast as 40 kph (25 miles per hour). They swim in all oceans but prefer polar waters.

◀ This giant sea spider has ten legs. It lives on the ocean floor near the South Pole. Sea spiders have between four and ten legs. They are not members of the same family group as land spiders, all of which have eight legs.

The bodies of sea spiders are so small that some of their food is digested in their legs!

PEOPLE OF THE POLES

On the icecap of Antarctica there are no human inhabitants. Only scientists brave these regions to carry out their experiments.

In the Arctic, however, local people have learned how to survive in the harsh climate. Many still live as **nomads**, following the herds of animals which provide their livelihood, although today many of them live in one of the settlements.

The Inuit, or Eskimo as they are sometimes known, live in North America and the USSR and are the largest group. Few still drive sleds

▼ Igloos are now mostly built as overnight resting places on long hunting trips. They are built from slabs of ice, carefully cut to size and placed together for a snug fit against the winds. Traditional lighting came from whale or seal oil burnt in a small container. This also heated the room efficiently.

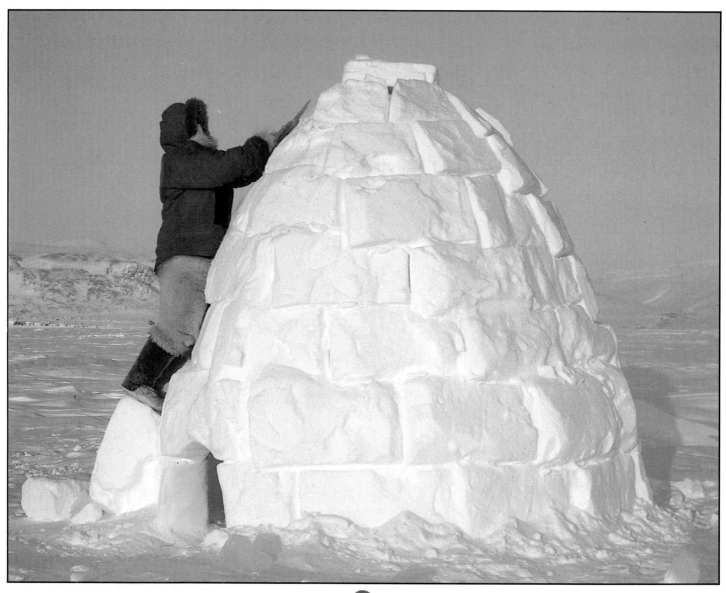

pulled by husky dogs, or wear the traditional stitched animal skins. Most prefer to ride over the icecap on engine-driven snowmobiles, and to wear anoraks, although the stitched skins are, in fact, even warmer.

Today the closely related Inuit tribes of Alaska and the Soviet Union are allowed to meet without regard to political boundaries. Recent changes in the way that Eastern Europe is governed means that people living there are now able to visit other countries more freely than under the old laws.

The people of the North may in future find it easier to fish and hunt where the animals wander and not where governments force them to live.

PEOPLE FACTS

The Yahgans and Onas peoples who used to live in the Antarctic region at the tip of South America, have today died out.

Arctic people eat mostly fish and meat, as there is little plant life available.

More than 100,000 Inuit are spread over four countries along the Arctic coastline.

▲ An Inuit man wearing his traditional costume of boots, leggings, trousers, hooded jacket, and mitts. These are made from the skins of animals such as caribou, bear, or wolf. The clothes are made loose-fitting to allow an extra layer of warm air around the wearer. The seams are tightly sewn to waterproof the garment.

WATCHING THE WEATHER

Polar lands are a particularly useful place to study the weather because the temperature at the Poles affects the climate all over the world. It is the cold air blowing from the Poles and meeting the hot air from the equator that causes our weather patterns. Scientists can also find out about patterns in the world's climate

▼ This map shows major cities around the world that will be in serious danger of being submerged by the sea if the polar icecaps melt as a result of global warming. Even world centers like London or New York would be lost beneath the waters.

THE EARTH'S ATMOSPHERE

ionosphere

stratosphere

troposphere

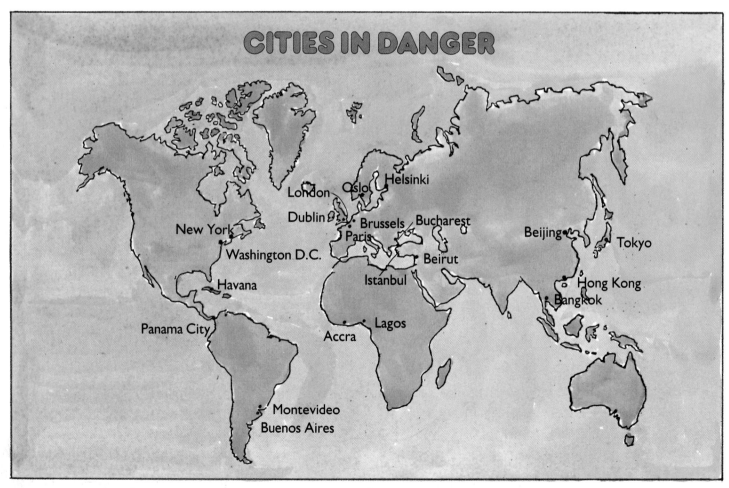

CITIES IN DANGER

Helsinki
Oslo
London
Dublin
New York
Brussels
Bucharest
Paris
Beijing
Tokyo
Washington D.C.
Beirut
Havana
Istanbul
Hong Kong
Bangkok
Panama City
Lagos
Accra
Montevideo
Buenos Aires

thousands of years ago by studying the ice which has lain at the Poles since that time.

Many scientists believe that the world is warming up, for a number of reasons. Chief among these is the fact that there is a growing hole in the **ozone layer** at each Pole where it is thickest. This is the layer of the earth's atmosphere that protects us from the harmful ultraviolet rays of the sun. The ozone is being destroyed by man-made chemicals including chlorofluorocarbons (CFCs) which are used in aerosol sprays.

Global warming is also increased by the effect of the **greenhouse gases**. Gases produced by industrial

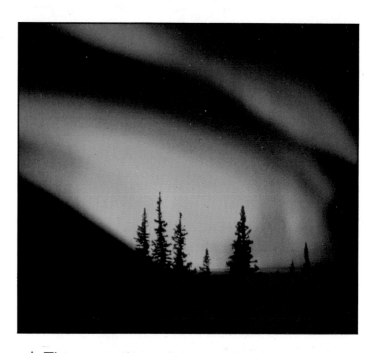

▲ The aurora borealis is a beautiful and rare sight seen mainly near the North pole. It is caused by the entry of solar particles into the earth's magnetic field. A similar phenomenon in the Antarctic is known as the aurora australis.

HOW YOU CAN HELP THE WORLD

● Give up using aerosols which contain CFCs. Look for alternatives. Dry-cleaning solvents also contain CFCs, so when buying clothes, choose those that are washable.

● Ask adults to think of different ways to get rid of garden waste other than burning it. Chemicals in the smoke are carbons and help to pollute the atmosphere.

● Because trees hold large amounts of carbon dioxide that would otherwise be released into the atmosphere, join with your friends in a community effort to plant more trees.

processes are building up in the earth's atmosphere. These gases act as a blanket, trapping heat from the sun, instead of allowing it to be reflected back into space.

As the world grows warmer, so the oceans around the Poles are growing more hospitable. At present, polar temperatures rise only to 10°C (50°F) at the very height of summer. If the temperature were to rise by more than 5 percent at the Poles, the ice would melt and sea levels across the world could rise drastically. Low-lying cities, such as London and New York, as well as whole countries like the Netherlands and Bangladesh, could be flooded. At these temperatures many of the specialized animals and plants of the polar regions would die out too.

EXPLOITING THE POLES

The first outsiders to see potential for money-making in the Poles came during the nineteenth century. They killed whales in great numbers for their meat and for their blubber which was used in a variety of products from soap to oil. Seals, particularly fur seals, were trapped for their attractive pelts. Penguins were killed because their oil was useful as a light source.

Today international agreements are in force to protect the creatures of the Poles from hunting. A few animals are still killed each year for scientific purposes, and the local peoples are also permitted to hunt and kill a number of animals.

Animals face other dangers too. Polar bears are great scavengers and may become too dependent on scientific bases for scraps of food. They can often be seen in garbage dumps, where they sometimes eat unsuitable things, cut themselves on sharp edges, or lose the will to hunt.

Extra industrial activity at the Poles may also add to the world's environmental problems. The glaring white surface of the icecap at each Pole helps to reflect back into space hot rays from the sun.

Pale colors bounce rays of light off their surface. Bright, shiny snow is very good at doing this. Dark colors soak in warm rays of light and grow hotter. This is why you may prefer to wear light-colored clothes to help you stay cool in the hot summer.

POLAR RESOURCES

● 98% of Antarctica lies covered by thick ice, but beneath may lie valuable deposits of rubies and other minerals.

● Reserves of oil and natural gas lie under Alaska, Arctic Canada, and Siberia. Further oil deposits are found off the coast of Greenland, on the Arctic shores of the North Atlantic, and in parts of the Southern Ocean.

● Oil spillage from a tanker accident in Alaska in the spring of 1989 caused the death of many birds and other animals.

◀ The bleached white bones of long-dead whales remind us of the years when the great mammals were hunted mercilessly. The bowhead was even called the "right" whale because it was so easy to catch.

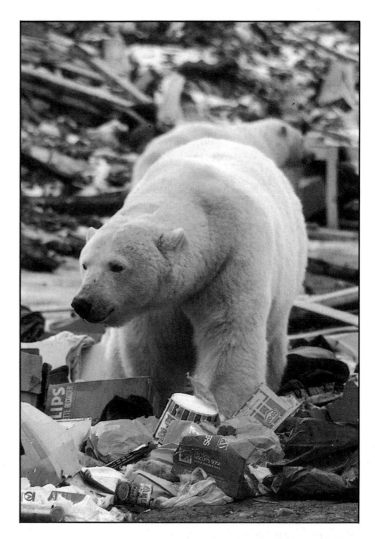

▲ A polar bear forages among the discarded litter of a modern settlement in northern Canada. He may be poisoned or injured and also poses a serious threat to local inhabitants.

Some scientists fear that dust and grime from industrial processes might make the ice darker and therefore reflect fewer rays than at present. This would trap heat in the earth's atmosphere and increase the effects of global warming.

If people attempt to melt the permafrost to mine for minerals and other resources there may also be the danger that modern structures such as buildings, railways, or vital oil-relaying pipelines will subside, and be ruined.

SAVING THE POLES

It is important that human beings realize the importance of keeping the polar lands clean for the future. The specialized animals and plants will die if temperatures are allowed to rise.

Sensible measures have been taken to establish both North and South Poles as areas of especial scientific interest rather than purely as areas to be exploited. The first legal restraint on animal slaughter in these regions was passed by Britain in 1904. Since then many other nations have joined to save threatened species.

The long-standing Antarctic Treaty concerning ownership of the lands of the South Pole was agreed upon by most of the world's governments.

Even industry has taken steps to avoid further damage to this most desolate of the world parks. Special ice roads have been built to protect slow-growing plants from being crushed under the wheels of a succession of heavy vehicles.

Similarly, oil and gas pipelines are built raised from the ground like bridges. Despite people's continuing encroachment on the lands of the Poles, the caribou in the North may continue their migration in peace.

▲ A rookery of king penguins shows the efficiency of creatures that have adapted to extreme conditions. If the Poles become warmer, they may not survive.

▶ An aerial view of the snow-crusted ridges of Greenland. The world would lose one of its great natural beauties if we allow the destruction of the polar icecaps.

CROW STEALS SOME DAYLIGHT

For thousands of years people have told stories about the world around them. Often these stories try to explain something that people do not really understand, like how the world began, or where light comes from. This tale is told by the Inuit people who live in the polar lands of Northern Canada.

Long ago, in the northern lands where the Inuit live, there was no daylight. The people ate, slept, went hunting, and cooked, all in darkness. There was no light to tell the people which was day and which was night, so they all got up at different times. When they needed to see they

day he told them about a land where light shone all day and people could see without using a lamp and could spot animals far off. The villagers were amazed at this and began to realize how difficult their lives were without light during the daytime.

would light little seal-oil lamps which gave off a small glimmer of light, scarcely enough to see by.

In one village lived a wise old Crow. He used to tell the people stories of the far-off lands that he had visited. One

"When we go fishing," said one, "we have to shine a light into the holes we make in the ice to see if any fish are there and that scares the fish off. If it were light all the time we would be able to see the fish before they saw us."

"And without light," said another, "we are quite likely to walk straight into the arms of a polar bear before we even realize that it's there. If it were light all the time, we would be able to see them in the distance and keep away."

All the villagers begged the Crow to go to the land of daylight and fetch them some light. At first the Crow said no, because it was such a long journey. But the villagers had always been very good to him, so eventually he agreed.

It was a very long journey indeed and when, at last, the Crow reached the eastern lands where the sky was bright with daylight, he sank to the ground, exhausted. He found himself in a village not so very different from the one he had left. In the middle of the village was a house from which daylight shone brightly.

"Aha!" thought the Crow. "That is where the daylight comes from."

As he watched, a woman walked up to the house. The Crow flew over to the door, shook off his skin and turned himself into a speck of dust, which settled on the woman's dress as she went into the house.

Inside the house a great chief sat watching a baby playing on a fur rug. As the woman passed she bent down and tickled the baby. She didn't notice the tiny speck of dust fall from her dress and into the little baby's ear. It was the Crow of course!

The baby tugged at its ear, which tickled dreadfully, and began to cry, whereupon the chief and the woman leapt up and began to fuss over it.

"Ask for some daylight," whispered the speck of dust.

So the baby cried for some daylight. The chief picked up a carved wooden box, placed it before the baby and opened the lid. Inside were seven glowing balls of daylight. The chief took out one of the balls and gave it to the baby. The baby was so delighted with its new toy that all its tears were gone at once.

"Ask for a string to be tied to the ball," whispered the speck of dust in the baby's ear.

And the baby began to cry for a string to be tied to the beautiful ball of daylight.

No sooner had the chief tied a string to the ball and given it to the baby, than the little speck of dust whispered in the baby's ear again.

"Move over to the doorway."

The baby crawled over to the hut's doorway, trailing the ball of daylight on its string and sat, framed by the arch, with daylight shining brightly all around.

Gradually the baby moved further and further out of the house, dangling the ball, right to the very spot where the Crow had left his skin. Quick as a flash, the speck of dust fell out of the baby's ear, picked up the skin, and became the Crow again. The Crow snatched the string from the baby and flew off, carrying away the bright ball of daylight.

The baby began to scream and cry,

and all the villagers came rushing out of their houses. They threw stones at the Crow and tried to shoot him down with their bows and arrows but the Crow flew off towards the west much too fast for them.

When, at last, the Crow came to the land of the Inuit, he broke off a piece of daylight from the ball over each village that he passed and let it fall. Finally, after much traveling, he reached the village that he had set off from. Then he let go of the string and all that was left of the ball of daylight fell to the ground and shattered. Shafts of light streamed into all the houses. The villagers rushed out of their houses to thank the Crow for his wonderful gift.

The Crow told the story of how he had stolen the light and explained to all the villagers that he had not brought enough light for them to have daylight all the time, but only enough for daylight half the year, and that the other half of the year they would have darkness.

"But if I had brought enough daylight for it to be always light," he said, "You would have had as much trouble as you did when it was always dark!"

TRUE OR FALSE?

Which of these facts are true and which ones are false? If you have read this book carefully, you will know the answers.

1. Summer falls between May and July at both Poles.

2. No plants grow in the polar lands.

3. Plants and animals once lived in a warmer climate on Antarctica.

4. The Arctic was named by the Ancient Greeks after the constellation of the Plough.

5. The Norwegian Roald Amundsen was the first man to reach the South Pole.

6. *The Titanic* sank in 1912 after running into a blue whale.

7. Large fragments from the ice sheet are called bergy growlers.

8. The largest permanent residents on the Antarctic ice sheet are insects.

9. A male emperor penguin will go as long as four months without food.

10. Polar bear cubs are born two at a time.

11. Arctic people are mostly vegetarian.

12. Planting trees is one way to reduce the amount of carbon dioxide in the atmosphere.

GLOSSARY

● **Baleen whales** have a curtain of bony plates in their mouths. These allow them to sift the tiny krill from the ocean, on which they feed.

● **Bergy bits** are large sections that have broken off the ice sheet.

● **Blubber** is the name for the thick layer of fat on animals such as seals, walruses, penguins and whales. This layer helps to protect them against the cold. In the past it was used to make goods such as soap and oil for household lighting.

● **Brash ice** is the name for small fragments of ice.

● **Camouflage** is used by animals to hide themselves in their surroundings. For example, the coat of an Arctic fox is white and makes it invisible against the snow, from a distance. Camouflage helps to protect an animal from predators and helps it capture prey.

● **Carnivores** are meat-eating animals.

● **Frazil ice** is the first thin ice that forms as the sea begins to freeze.

● **Germination** is the moment when plant seeds are roused from their dormant state by suitable conditions for growth and begin to sprout.

● **Glacier** is a river of ice that moves very slowly, pushed by new ice that forms on high ground.

● **Greenhouse gases** such as carbon dioxide collect in the Earth's atmosphere. They trap the heat rays from the Sun and prevent them from bouncing back into outer space. Because of this the Earth's climate is changing and growing warmer.

● **Growlers** are small pieces that have broken off the ice sheet.

● **Herbivores** are plant-eating animals.

● **Iceberg** is a large lump of ice that floats in the sea. Many icebergs break off from the ends of glaciers that slowly pour into the sea. Only one-tenth of these icebergs usually shows above the surface of the water.

● **Icecap** is a name for the huge shield of ice that covers both the Arctic Ocean and Antarctica.

● **Ice flowers** form when salt is pushed out as the sea freezes. The salt forms strange arrangements of beautiful crystals.

● **Ice sheet** is another name for the Arctic and Antarctic shields of ice.

● **Incubation** is the time between the laying of a bird's egg and its hatching.

● **Meltwater** is the water that appears when ice and snow melt during the polar summer. In some areas meltwater can cause flooding.

● **Nomads** are tribespeople who do not have a settled home. Instead they follow their herds of animals, in search of fresh pasture. The Lapps of northern Scandinavia travel in this way, tending their reindeer.

● **Ozone layer** prevents harmful ultraviolet rays from the sun from entering the earth's atmosphere. A hole in this layer is forming over each Pole where it is thickest.

● **Pack ice** is formed when slabs of thick sea ice freeze together.

● **Pancake ice** is created when the salt is pushed out of freezing sea water. It often forms in round shapes with raised edges, like pancakes.

● **Pelt** is a name for an animal's fur.

● **Permafrost** is an underground layer of soil that remains frozen all year, even during the polar summer.

● **Plates** are huge sections in the earth's crust on which the continents float. These plates move slowly over hundreds of thousands of years. The continents move with them. As the plates meet and their edges grind against each other, volcanoes erupt and earthquakes occur.

● **Subarctic** describes the area south of the Arctic which is almost as cold in winter but much warmer in summer.

● **Tabular icebergs** have a large flat surface: like that of a table.

● **Toothed whales** have peglike teeth on their lower jaws. They eat animals such as seals, squid, and fish.

● **Treeline** is the furthest point to the north, beyond which the climate is too inhospitable for trees to grow.

● **Tundra** is the belt of land between the Arctic ice sheet and the treeline. Rough scrub is the only vegetation here.

INDEX

albatross   13
animals   10,11
Antarctica   7
Antarctic Treaty   22
Arctic Ocean   6
Arctic redpoll   12
Arctic tern   12
aurora australis, borealis   19

caribou   7
climate   6

deep-sea angler   14
duck: eider   12
    teal   12
    widgeon   12

Europe, northern   6
explorers   7

glacier   8
greenhouse gases   19
Greenland   22,23

history   7

ice-fish   14
iceberg   5,8
igloo   16
International Ice Patrol   8
Inuit   16,17

krill   14

lark   12
lemming   10

midnight Sun   4

North America   6

Onas   16
ozone layer   18,19

penguins: 10,12
    emperor   12
    king   12,22
permafrost   6,21
pipit   12
plants   5
polar bear   10,20
ptarmigan   12
puffin   13

raven   12
resources   20

seals   10,20
sea spider   14,15
shrew   10
snowy owl   12
Soviet Union   6,17
stoat   11
summer   4,12

Titanic, The   8
treeline   6
tundra   6

weather   18,19
whales: blue   15
    bowhead (right)   20,21
winter   12
wolf   11

Yahgan   16